A Believer's Guide to Network Marketing

Ahesha Catalano

A Team Press

No part of this book may be reproduced or transmitted in any form or by any means, electronic or mechanical, including photocopying, recording, or by an information storage and retrieval system–except by a reviewer who may quote brief passages in a review to be printed in a magazine, newspaper, or on the web–without permission in writing from the Publisher.

For more information, please contact:
A Team Press
info@ateampress.info

Printed and bound in the United States of America
All rights reserved.

ISBN:9780991044016

Preface

So many people are selling their secret to success, their plan for your promotion. With the purest of intentions, you would probably jump "all in" only to find yourself no further along than when you started. Maybe you would have a few new insights to things you already knew, with a few "Ah-ha" moments sprinkled here and there, but that would be about it. This book makes no such claim. I have no answers. I promise no unveiled secret. This book is a simple companion to the greatest book, an organized compilation of some of the scriptures that have helped me along this journey, on which I am still a focused traveler. I simply invite you along during my journey and share the thoughts that keep me strong.

Table of Contents
I New to Network Marketing
II New People Join Your Team
III People Quit or Customers Fall Off
IV Dry Season
V Fear
VI Networking with Others
VII Team Issues
VIII Leaders
IX Negative People
X Promotion
XI Parting Words
XII Excuses Be Gone: Affirmations that will retrain your brain

I New to Network Marketing

Always remember that when you give your life and commit your business to the Lord, situations and circumstances could work out in ways that are beyond anything you ever could have imagined. Get ready for the ride of your life.

Matthew 6: 33 But seek ye first the kingdom of God, and his righteousness; and all these things shall be added unto you.

There is no better way than this to begin anything. Short, sweet and to the point. If your heart is pure and your intentions are good, if the Lord God is first and foremost in your life, He should certainly be at the vanguard of your business. If you seek to please God in all that you do, He will surely bless you in some way.

Matthew 5: 16 Let your light so shine before men, that they may see your good works, and glorify your Father which is in heaven.

No matter what you do, no matter what happens from this point forward, remember this verse. In sharing your message, your products, your services or your brand, you want to be a light in the world. Business is all about the relationships you build. You want people to think of you as a light, as someone who can help them solve a problem, fix an issue or improve something personally or professionally. Stay positive. Stay consistent. Be a light as you go out into this world of darkness. Keep your mind focused on the fact that

God brought you to where you are for a reason. Don't let anyone steal your joy or dim your light.

Psalm 37:5 Commit thy way unto the Lord; trust also in him; and he shall bring it to pass.

"Commitment is doing the thing you said you would do, long after the mood you said it in has left you," - Anonymous. Keep this in mind as you go about the business or learning and developing your business. Stick with it. When the novelty wears off and the dust clears, it is time to get busy. Once the honeymoon stage is over, persevere and continue to commit all aspects of your personal and professional life to God so that He can bring to pass all that He has in store for you.

Proverbs 16: 3 Commit thy works unto the Lord, and thy thoughts shall be established.

Taking on any new venture, especially in business, can be a daunting task. The key ingredient in success is mindset. With the proper mindset, an individual can expect to be successful regardless of any circumstances. For even in the "unwanted" situation, a victorious thinker will see the lesson in the mess. They will prepare their testimony in the middle of the test, making them ultimately successful, even if things didn't end up as they thought they would in the beginning. So, you see, it is all about mindset. Once you take a step on the path that God lead you to, commit your works to Him. Allow him to keep your mind focused and clear. Trust him to establish your thoughts.

Galatians 6:10 As we have therefore opportunity, let us do good unto all men, especially unto them who are of the household of faith.

You are in business with people, for people. That could be awesome or awful for you, depending on how you look at it. Good, bad or indifferent, it is your responsibility to do right by them all. Your existing and potential customers and business partners are counting on you and your knowledge. Treat them well, even those who do not share your vision. Keep your heart pure and share your message. Let your life be the light that guides people into your business and closer to the Lord.

1 Corinthians 14:12 Even so you, since you are zealous for spiritual gifts, let it be for the edification of the church that you seek to excel.

Enough said. We are the church, each and every one of us, as followers of Jesus Christ. In all that you do, you should strive to be a blessing to someone else. To take the call of duty a step further, we should desire to be a blessing to both believers and nonbelievers, so that our life can be an example of the love of Jesus.

II New People Join Your Team

Sharing your opportunity or products and services can be as difficult, and yet as rewarding, as sharing the gospel. After all, shouldn't you consider an opportunity that affords the average individual a chance to experience financial freedom good news? Know that while you will face persecution and ridicule for thinking outside of the box, it will all be worth it in the end, if you make it count. Recognize and appreciate the great responsibility that lies ahead of you.

Hebrews 13:17 Obey them that have the rule over you, and submit yourselves: for they watch for your souls, as they that must give account, that they may do it with joy, and not with grief: for that is unprofitable for you.

As individuals take that giant leap of faith to partner with you in business, you must not take that for granted. Much of what you have done to achieve the level of success you have attained involved following a system. Show your new business partner how to do the same. As you build an organization of like-minded individuals, if they happen to be follows of the gospel of Jesus Christ, they should desire to, and see the value in, placing their business in your hands; not that you will do the work for them, but that they trust you to show them the way. Having said that, the second portion of the verse is equally important. When you sponsor new reps into your business, you should wholeheartedly feel that their success is in your hands (to the degree that they are willing to follow the system, of course). Be sure to lead the horses to the water and remove as many obstacles as possible along the way. I do so with the utmost joy. Anything less than that would be unprofitable for them, and ultimately for you.

Ephesians 2:10 For we are His workmanship, created in Christ Jesus for good works, which God prepared beforehand that we should walk in them.

No matter how you came into your current business opportunity, please know that there is no such thing as a coincidence for a believer. We all have a purpose. We can alter the course of our lives to the degree that we are willing to ask, seek and knock. Just remember that to keep God in the center of all of your endeavors.

Romans 12: 2 And do not be conformed to this world, but be transformed by the renewing of your mind, that you may prove what is that good and acceptable and perfect will of God.

Network marketing. I cannot think of a more fitting environment or circumstance that requires a renewed mind. Unless you belong to a family of network marketers, chances are you have encountered more than one of two critics. Everyone knows someone who is a self-proclaimed network marketing failure, someone who boldly decrees, "those things don't work". Unfortunately, very few people know someone who has hung in there, beat the odds, followed the system and made network marketing work for them. If you continue to talk to or associate with individuals in the former category, you will survive, so long as you adopt a renewed mind. Stay in the word and continue to meditate on God's promises for your life, and not the worries and concerns of individuals who barely have control over their own lives. Place your business in the hands of the Lord, not in man, and definitely not individuals who have never done what you aspire to do and couldn't show you the way with a lamp, map and GPS combined.

II Peter 1: 5-11 But also for this very reason, giving all diligence, add to your faith virtue, to virtue knowledge, 6 to knowledge self-control, to self-control perseverance, to perseverance godliness, 7 to godliness brotherly kindness, and to brotherly kindness love. 8 For if these things are yours and abound, you will be neither barren nor unfruitful in the knowledge of our Lord Jesus Christ. 9For he who lacks these things is shortsighted, even to blindness, and has forgotten that he was cleansed from his old sins. 10Therefore, brethren, be even more diligent to make your call and election sure, for if you do these things you will never stumble; 11for so an entrance will be supplied to you abundantly into the everlasting kingdom of our Lord and Savior Jesus Christ.

What a recipe for success! Let's check the ingredients: diligence, faith, virtue, knowledge, self-control, perseverance, godliness, brotherly kindness and love. Add each characteristic to your business model. Let your work and words reflect them all. Be a Godly leader.

2 Thessalonians 1:3 We are bound to thank God always for you, brethren, as it is fitting, because your faith grows exceedingly, and the love of every one of you all abounds toward each other.

Keep this in mind as new individuals patronize your business or join your team. Love them as Jesus love you. Be grateful for them. Pray for them. Your love for them shows and affirms your faith in God that He will provide, that everything will work out fine. And if, by chance or design, depending on how you look at it, things do not work out in a way that feels good or pleasant to you, your actions and attitude should reflect your faith and trust in God and His plan. Remember that *obstacles are opportunities to exercise your faith.*

Luke 6:38 Give, and it will be given to you: good measure, pressed down, shaken together, and running over will be put into your bosom. For with the same measure that you use, it will be measured back to you."

Be willing to give of yourself for your new partners. Don't assume that they know the way or will figure things out for themselves, even if they have prior success in other professional areas. Take them under your wing and lead by example. You will be blessed to the degree that you are willing to give.

Colossians 3:23 And whatever you do, do it heartily, as to the Lord and not to men.

We all know the Golden Rule, which tells us to treat others as we would like to be treated. Taken a step further, how different would your interactions with others be if you treated them all as you would Jesus Christ himself? Seek first to understand others, without regard for being understood. Give without expectation. Practice forgiveness and love others as Christ loves us.

III People Quit or Customers Fall Off

Just as sure as some people will join you in your entrepreneurial endeavors or patronize your business, there are many more who will not. There are still some who may join you for a short time, however long their season may be. Press on and do your best regardless.

Romans 12:11 Never be lazy, but work hard and serve the Lord enthusiastically.

People are going to quit. Customers will fall off. The sooner you realize those two things, the better off you will be. The Lord God is a provider unlike any other. Just as Jesus Christ raised the dead, He alone can resurrect your business. So despite what happens in your business, as it pertains to other people, continue to follow the systems that brought you success initially. Continue to serve the Lord with an enthusiastic heart and trust that whatever is done in His name will be blessed at just the right time.

Jeremiah 17:7 But blessed are those who trust in the Lord and have made the Lord their hope and confidence.

All that glitters is not gold. Try not to get caught up in the BSOs (bright, shiny objects) associated with anything of this world. Maintain unwavering faith, hope and trust in God and God alone.

Ephesians 4:2 Always be humble and gentle. Be patient with each other, making allowance for each other's faults because of your love.

Patience is key. Sometimes people are comfortable sharing their situations and circumstances. Other times, they are not. Whether you know the back-story or you don't, the situations will remain the same. So it may not be wise to concern yourself with the details. Be grateful for the business partners and customers you have and those you had. Always focus on obtaining new customers and showing the existing customers that they are appreciated.

Job 1:21 He said, "I came naked from my mother's womb, and I will be naked when I leave. The Lord gave me what I had, and the Lord has taken it away. Praise the name of the Lord!"

Keep your heart and mind focused on what is important. People change. Things fade. Yet, the love of the Lord remains the same yesterday, today and always. Regardless of the changes you may see in your business, maintain your unwavering faith in the Lord that what God has for you is yours and yours alone.

Isaiah 40:29 He gives power to the weak and strength to the powerless.

There will be times when you feel weak and powerless. Psalm 30:5 teaches us that "weeping may endure for a night, but joy cometh in the morning." How long that "night" will be in our life or in your business is up to the Lord above.

Psalm 34:18 The LORD is close to the brokenhearted and saves those who are crushed in spirit.

Some of the things that happen to you are meant to build you up. Some things are meant to teach you a lesson. Still other things may arise in your life so that you can endure the experience only to minister to others. No matter what, try not to let your spirit be crushed. Seek to understand the lesson that is present. However, if at all your spirit is under the attack of your flesh and you feel your light diminished, know that the Lord is close. If you keep your mind focused on God and His word, and commit your plans to Him, He will grant you the desires of your heart. Just remember that He is close in all times, especially those times of need.

Matthew 6:25 "That is why I tell you not to worry about everyday life—whether you have enough food and drink, or enough clothes to wear. Isn't life more than food, and your body more than clothing?

God will always provide for us, according to His will. That should be more than enough encouragement for you. Worry and faith cannot exist in the same mind at the same time. So replace every negative, worrisome thought with three positive, unwavering, faithful thoughts of how God will handle everything.

IV Dry Season

In the microwave society we live in, it has become commonplace to want what you want when you want it. Everyone wants everything NOW, if not yesterday. In business and in life, we must remember to control what we can (our thoughts and actions) and leave the rest up to the Lord. Let Him work out the circumstances and details. Things will change exactly when and how they are supposed to.

Ecclesiastes 3:1-2 1To every thing there is a season, and a time to every purpose under the heaven. 2A time to be born, and a time to die; a time to plant, and a time to pluck up that which is planted.

Don't be discouraged when individuals who were initially on your team or patronizing your business are no longer doing so. Either it was because of you or because of them. So you are left with two choices. If you are somehow the reason for the discontinuing of their connection with you, figure out what you need to change or improve and do so. If they have moved on for reasons that have nothing to do with you, recognize that their season is over.

Get over it as quickly as possible and move forward.

Proverbs 3:5-6 5Trust in the Lord with all thine heart; and lean not unto thine own understanding. 6In all thy ways acknowledge him, and he shall direct thy paths.

It is so easy to buy your own press and think that you have it all figured out when things go well, only to become depressed and anxious when things do not go your way. Instead, put your faith, hope and trust in God in all things, so that your steps may be ordered according to Him will for your life.

Hebrews 11:1 Now faith is the substance of things hoped for, the evidence of things not seen.

Once you decide in your mind that you will be successful, that abundance is available to you and rightfully yours, that's it. End of story. Trust that the Lord will provide. Hold onto your unshakable faith that things will work out in your favor, no matter how long it takes, no matter how many no's you hear. Know that with the Lord on your side, you will win.

James 1:4 But let patience have her perfect work, that ye may be perfect and entire, wanting nothing.

All things take time. Your business venture is no exception. When you find joy in the journey, when you appreciate the process, you want for nothing because you know that it is only a matter of time before your reaping season comes.

Hebrews 13:5 Let your conversation be without covetousness; and be content with such things as ye have: for he hath said, I will never leave thee, nor forsake thee.

Lao Tzu said, "Watch your thoughts; they become words. Watch your words; they become actions. Watch your actions; they become habit. Watch your habits; they become character. Watch your character; it becomes your destiny." When you covet the position and possessions of others, you call attention to what you lack. Know that thoughts become things and you bring about what you think about intently. You must ask yourself if it is worth it. What is more important, what you would like to have or what others currently have? You goals and dreams must be so important to you that you refuse to waste time thinking about where others are in their journey. Trust and believe that you will have your time exactly when and how you are supposed to. Focus on the love of the Lord and know that He will provide.

Psalm 145:18-19 The Lord is nigh unto all them that call upon him, to all that call upon him in truth. 19He will fulfill the desire of them that fear him: he also will hear their cry, and will save them.

No matter where you are in life, no matter how things may appear on the surface, know that the Lord God Almighty is near. He is with you during every phase of your journey. Call on Him anytime. Know that things will work out for your good, even if it doesn't seem to be so at the moment.

Psalm 126:5 They that sow in tears shall reap in joy.

As you work hard in your business, as you grow to develop your skills and abilities, there will be difficult times. You may experience sleepless nights and frustrating mornings. Stay committed to your goals and focused on the promised of God. If you continue to sow the right seeds, you will reap the blessings that are in store for you.

Galatians 6:9 And let us not be weary in well doing: for in due season we shall reap, if we faint not.

It is important to remember a small word in this scripture... "if". In due season, we shall reap IF we faint not. IF you give up on your dreams and goals before you have reached your goal, you will not the blessing you initially sought. Do not give up. Hang in there because your season will come.

1 Corinthians 15:58 Therefore, my beloved brethren, be ye steadfast, unmovable, always abounding in the work of the Lord, forasmuch as ye know that your labor is not in vain in the Lord.

When you step out on faith, you have to commit to staying the course. Success in any business venture will not come without hard work and determination. Approach your business and all that you do as though it is the work of the Lord, and you will find a lesson and a blessing in all things, so that your work will not possibly be in vain.

V Fear

Fear is the absolute opposite of faith. The two cannot possibly exist simultaneously. Knowing this should help you through fearful times. When you are cognizant of fearful feelings, forgive yourself because it is a human emotion that cannot be avoided. Remember that your faith has more power than any fear. Trust and know that most of what you fear will never come to fruition anyway. Then, make certain to take action, no matter how small, in the direction of your dreams.

Psalm 27:1 The Lord is my light and my salvation; whom shall I fear? The Lord is the strength of my life; of whom shall I be afraid?

Anytime thoughts of fear enter your mind, let this verse come flooding in like a tidal wave, eradicating anything that does not resemble ultimate faith in the Lord's ability to do miraculous works. The same God that raised Lazarus from the dead can protect you from whatever comes your way. Concern yourself only with what stands before you in the moment, and trust that regardless of what it is, the Lord will take of it on your behalf.

1 John 5:14 And we are confident that he hears us whenever we ask for anything that pleases him.

Throughout your business dealings, check yourself and your intentions. Would God agree that what you ask for is pleasing to Him? If so, persist in your efforts. If not, there is no time like the present to shift your focus.

Psalm 18:32 God arms me with strength, and he makes my way perfect.

This verse does not say the way will be made easy. Nor does it say the way will be made comfortable or pleasant. It reads "perfect", perfect according to the Lord. After all, why shouldn't it be according to God's definition of perfection? After all, the bible says the Lord will arm you with strength. There should be no further worry regarding "the way". It matters none what it looks like, how long it is, where it starts or where it ends. The way will be made perfect and you are already equipped with everything you need to be victorious.

Job 11:13-18 13 If only you would prepare your heart and lift up your hands to him in prayer! 14 Get rid of your sins, and leave all iniquity behind you. 15 Then your face will brighten with innocence. You will be strong and free of fear. 16 You will forget your misery; it will be like water flowing away. 17 Your life will be brighter than the noonday. Even darkness will be as bright as morning. 18 Having hope will give you courage. You will be protected and will rest in safety.

Take each verse one at a time and let the words migrate deep into your spirit. The power of prayer is magnificent. If you do not already do so, begin to pray over your company, your business, your customers and your partners every single day. Try not to commit sin. Yet, if such should occur, do not pass up the opportunity to repent and forgive yourself. Trust in the Lord that you will be victorious, that there will be light at the end of the tunnel of your life and your business. If you learn to count your blessings every day, you won't even have to wait until the end to enjoy it.

Psalm 46:1 God is our refuge and strength, always ready to help in times of trouble.

How can you possibly give into fear with the King of king and Lord of lords as your refuge and strength? Call upon Him. Rest in His comfort. Read his promises for your life and know that you were created for greatness. Don't sweat the small things or allow them to shift your focus. You have an omnipotent, omnipresent savior ready, willing and able to comfort you.

Psalm 28:7 The Lord is my strength and shield. I trust him with all my heart. He helps me, and my heart is filled with joy. I burst out in songs of thanksgiving.

The more time you spend as an entrepreneur, the more worries and fear that may arise for you. Arm yourself with the word of God and anything else you need to keep your mind clear, focused and optimistic. Music and praise will always do the trick. The next time fear creeps in, count your blessings and let out a shout of praise. Put on your favorite inspirational music and release whatever you are holding onto.

Exodus 4:10-12 10 But Moses pleaded with the Lord, "O Lord, I'm not very good with words. I never have been, and I'm not now, even though you have spoken to me. I get tongue-tied, and my words get tangled." 11Then the Lord asked Moses, "Who makes a person's mouth? Who decides whether people speak or do not speak, hear or do not hear, see or do not see? Is it not I, the Lord? 12 Now go! I will be with you as you speak, and I will instruct you in what to say."

Get over yourself! Quit getting ready to get ready and STAY ready. Don't question God or second-guess yourself. Once it is in your mind or on your heart to share your blessing with someone, just do it. Step out on faith, open up your mouth and speak!

VI Networking with Others

We are here on this earth to experience life together with others. This journey is no different. As you share the gospel, and as you share information regarding your business opportunity, products or services, be mindful of your interactions with others.

1 Thessalonians 5:11 So encourage each other and build each other up, just as you are already doing.

Treat people with compassion and maintain high integrity. You reap what you sow in all things, so it is best that your actions and words toward other people reflect what you would like to have played out in your own life.

1 Peter 4:9 Use hospitality one to another without grudging.

You never know when you will require assistance or support from someone else. It is difficult for many people to humble themselves and seek help from others in professional situations. So, if someone thinks highly of you or respects your opinion enough to ask anything of you, treat them with hospitality without reluctance. Network marketing is an industry that is all about people. Network within your company and with individuals in other companies and professions as well. You may be surprised at ways you can be a blessing to others and whom God uses to be a blessing to you.

Proverbs 27:17 As iron sharpens iron, so a man sharpens the countenance of his friend.

It is said that you are know by the company you keep. As the proverb goes, "A chain is only as strong as it's weakest link." In the beginning stages of any entrepreneurial journey, it is easy to feel as though some support is better than none at all. Such may not always be the case. You want to be sure that you are spending time and working with the right individuals. Be the iron that sharpens those around you. On the opposite end, you want to be sure that those around you enhance your life in some way as well. Choose your associations wisely.

Ecclesiastes 10:12 Wise words bring approval, but fools are destroyed by their own words.

First impressions are very important. Even if changes are made down the road, people rarely forget their initial encounter with a person. Be conscious of what you say and how you say things, during any time, but especially when networking with others. You business depends on your ability to master relationships with other people. Know the ins and outs of your product or service. Be honest about what you do and how you do it. Listen twice as much as you speak, and make your initial meeting more about learning about the other person than unleashing the floodgates of everything you do.

VII Team Issues

Everything happens for a reason. As such the people in your life are there for a reason. You can learn from they and they also stand to learn from you. Often times, people place that education in a box outside of themselves. Sometimes, those interactions we have with others show us exactly who and how we are.

Romans 12:14 Bless them which persecute you: bless, and curse not.

Along the way, you will have supporters in your corner, even from individuals who are not on your team or using your products or services. Cherish them and let them know they are appreciated whenever you can. For those who speak or plot against you, in public or in secret, bless them as well. For there is a lesson in all things. Figure out what their presence is supposed to teach you and move on with gratitude in your heart for a lesson learned.

Proverbs 22:5 Corrupt people walk a thorny, treacherous road; whoever values life will avoid it.

Honesty and integrity will take you far. Resist the temptations that may arise to gossip or be dishonest in any way. Avoid any conversations or actions that could cause your business, your image or your reputation to come crashing down around you.

Philippians 2:3 Let nothing be done through strife or vainglory; but in lowliness of mind let each esteem others better than themselves.

Many team issues are due to an inability to humble oneself. It is not a sign of weakness but of strength to humble oneself and edify another person, especially a person who has expertise in a particular area or field.

1 Thessalonians 5:14 Brothers and sisters, we urge you to warn those who are lazy. Encourage those who are timid. Take tender care of those who are weak. Be patient with everyone.

No one starts an entrepreneurial journey to babysit other adults who say they want to change their life. However, you must accept and understand that everyone will not have the same work ethic or goals as you. Lead the way, show them the ropes, but be will to accept that people must want to do for themselves. Work with the people who are willing and able to work with you for themselves. Just be willing to leave the door open for them to come to you when they are ready to step up their game and work harder.

Matthew 7:12 "Do to others whatever you would like them to do to you. This is the essence of all that is taught in the law and the prophets."

The essence of all that is taught by the prophets... Regardless of what is said to or about you, independent of whatever is done in your face or behind your back, you are to treat others as you wish to be treated.

Colossians 3:13 Make allowance for each other's faults, and forgive anyone who offends you. Remember, the Lord forgave you, so you must forgive others.

Unwillingness to forgive could ruin your business. People make mistakes. Things happen. Whether you continue a working relationship with someone who has offended you or not, you simply must forgive them and move on. If you are the party responsible for the wrongdoing, you must apologize and ask to be forgiven. Grudges and animosity have no place in a successful business or on a productive team. All parties involved must choose which is more important, the issue or the ultimate goal.

Proverbs 16:7 When people's lives please the Lord, even their enemies are at peace with them.

You cannot control what others say and do. All you can control is how you respond. God will hold you accountable for your words and actions in this life. No stories or excuses will be accepted. After all, He is all seeing, all-knowing. Let you life be an example of God's love. Jesus loved even those who crucified Him. Worry more about pleasing God and less about those who have wronged you. He will handle them as He sees fit.

Romans 14:19 Let us therefore follow after the things which make for peace, and things wherewith one may edify another.

As a leader, you have so many responsibilities. In network marketing, of course you want to be successful and build your business. However, you cannot lose sight of the fact that the only way you can truly be successful is in helping others, Whether they are customers or business partners who have joined you for this entrepreneurial journey, you cannot get it done without the help and support of others. So remain focused on ruining a peaceful business, remembering to model support, encouragement and acknowledgement of others and for others.

VIII Leaders

1 Corinthians 14:33 For God is not a God of disorder but of peace, as in all the meetings of God's holy people.

If there is disorder and confusion amongst your team, know that such should not be the case amongst God's holy people. We are human and surely do not behave as though we are holy at all times. If ever there are times of dissension, use it as an opportunity for growth and lead by example. Seek first to understand those involved and engage in meaningful dialogue with a unified intention to grow and come out stronger and wiser in the end.

1 Timothy 4:12 Don't let anyone think less of you because you are young. Be an example to all believers in what you say, in the way you live, in your love, your faith, and your purity.

No matter your age, as Christians and as leaders, it is extremely important to let your life (not your words) speak for you. Such is especially true if you or leaders in your organization are not aged in years or experience. Nevertheless, be the leader that you are called to be, and if you are living and working in accordance to God's word and His will, the rest will be taken care of, even the situations that arise just as life lessons for you.

Romans 12:17 Never pay back evil with more evil. Do things in such a way that everyone can see you are honorable.

No matter who or what tempts you, you owe it to everyone following your lead to be honorable. Vengeance does not belong to you. Since everyone reaps what he or she chooses to sow, don't waste precious time contemplating or acting on revenge. Let the Lord do what HE does, as the author or life as we know it. He can handle things far better than we can. Focus on your role as a leader and do let circumstances cause you to lead others astray by setting a poor example.

James 3:13 If you are wise and understand God's ways, prove it by living an honorable life, doing good works with the humility that comes from wisdom.

It is always easy to speak and do well when things are going well. In times of strife and dissension, it becomes far easier to give into the flesh and treat others as though we do not know any better. As the saying goes, "When you know better, you do better". So strive to know, do and be better. Treat all of your customers and business partners as though you have the wisdom and ability to handle any situation with a calm spirit and level head. Remember, others will do as you do, not as you say, so leave your team by example.

IX Negative People

If you are on this planet for any length of time passed your first earthly breath, chances are, you will encounter negative people at some point. As Wayne Dyer said, "How people treat you is their karma. How you respond is yours."

Romans 8:18 Yet what we suffer now is nothing compared to the glory he will reveal to us later.

Don't let the negative people around you steal your joy. Remember your rewards in heaven and limit the time you spend allowing the words and actions of negative people to affect you.

Psalm 39:10 But please stop striking me! I am exhausted by the blows from your hand.

Sometimes, you can feel completely knocked down while building your business. What is important is that you immediately get back up and allow Almighty God to fight the battle for you. Take one more step. Show up one more day. Your greatest victory could be just on the other side of what you thought was your greatest defeat.

Proverbs 12:2-3 2 The Lord approves of those who are good, but he condemns those who plan wickedness. 3 Wickedness never brings stability, but the godly have deep roots.

Make sure your intentions are good. Guard your mind against the temptation to plan wickedness.

Matthew 17:20 "You don't have enough faith," Jesus told them. "I tell you the truth, if you had faith even as small as a mustard seed, you could say to this mountain, 'Move from here to there,' and it would move. Nothing would be impossible."

*You absolutely **must** remember that everything works together for God's glory. If you truly trust and believe that, you will see that even negative people can have a positive impact on your life and your business. Those stumbling blocks in the form of negative people are just mountains. Tell them to move and have faith that they will, as soon as your lesson has been* learned. Pray for wisdom in dealing with them and be obedient to what is revealed to you.

Colossians 3:12 Since God chose you to be the holy people he loves, you must clothe yourselves with tenderhearted mercy, kindness, humility, gentleness, and patience.

What an awesome and mighty thing to be chosen by God! Let your life show how wonderful it is to be one of the chosen ones. Don't allow negative people separate you from your rightful position. Their issues simply are not worth it. Your thoughts and feelings toward your destiny must be so great that you refuse to be dragged down by someone else's negativity.

Proverbs 12:16 A fool is quick-tempered, but a wise person stays calm when insulted.

You must choose. Make the decision as to whether you want to be wise or a fool. There is no in-between and you cannot ride the fence on this one. Either be wise and maintain your cool or lose it and be the fool. The world may take your kindness for weakness, but you know otherwise. In standing your ground and standing up for yourself, just be sure to do so tactfully, with class and grace.

X Promotion

Network marketing can be such a tricky industry. A magnifying glass is held up to your personality traits, strengths and weakness, even before the money starts rolling in, and especially if you plan to build a sizeable organization. If you are a slacker, if will show in your business. If your people-skills are lacking, they must be improved if you plan to excel. Whatever you do well or whatever needs improvement will all be uncovered as something with which you must deal, as you rise to new heights, personally and professionally.

1 John 2: 15-16 15 Do not love this world nor the things it offers you, for when you love the world, you do not have the love of the Father in you. 16 For the world offers only a craving for physical pleasure, a craving for everything we see, and pride in our achievements and possessions. These are not from the Father, but are from this world

The money will come. The recognition will come. None of that will matter, nor will it satisfy if what you do does not glorify God and serve His will. Use your blessings to be a blessing, and don't allow money, fame or recognition to cloud your Godly judgment.

Psalm 9:1-2 I will praise you, Lord, with all my heart; I will tell of all the marvelous things you have done. 2I will be filled with joy because of you. I will sing praises to your name, O Most High.

Know that all you have and all that you are is thanks to the Lord God Almighty. Let that resonate in your mind, heart, words and deeds. Seize every opportunity to give God all the glory, honor and praise that you can, and never stop telling others of His abundant blessings on your life.

James 4:10 Humble yourselves before the Lord, and he will lift you up in honor.

Stay humble. Never think that you know it all or that you are any better than anyone else on the planet. Remember that every comment does not deserve a response and that you can be lifted up while lifting up others.

Psalm 62:10 Don't make a living by extortion or put your hope in stealing. And if your wealth increases, don't make it the center of your life.

Keep your thoughts and deeds focused on being a good steward of your time, talents and finances. Your commitment to serving the Lord should be more prevalent as your wealth increases, not less.

Hebrews 13:5 Don't love money; be satisfied with what you have. For God has said, "I will never fail you. I will never abandon you."

God is an awesome provider when we trust Him. Trust Him with all things large and small and have faith that He will meet your needs.

Colossians 3:23-24 23 Work willingly at whatever you do, as though you were working for the Lord rather than for people. 24 Remember that the Lord will give you an inheritance as your reward, and that the Master you are serving is Christ.

Don't get lost in tasks, titles, details, earthly rewards or anything and takes the focus off of where it ought to be. If things do not look as you would like them to at the moment, don't let it have a negative impact on your attitude. Continue to work for the Lord and know that the blessings are on the way.

Jeremiah 17:10 "But I, the Lord, search all hearts and examine secret motives. I give all people their due rewards, according to what their actions deserve."

You will be promoted in God's timing. Once you have learned all that there is to learn in the place where you are currently, once you have met those you were destined to meet, you will move onto where you are supposed to be. Just keep your heart and mind focused on the Lord and leave the rest to Him.

James 1:12 God blesses those who patiently endure testing and temptation. Afterward they will receive the crown of life that God has promised to those who love him.

The key words here are patiently and testing. The purpose of a test it so assess understanding. Know this and seek the lesson in all challenges. Endure the process, not begrudgingly, but with a pure heart of understanding.

Luke 16:10 "If you are faithful in little things, you will be faithful in large ones. But if you are dishonest in little things, you won't be honest with greater responsibilities."

We are referred to as the children of God. This verse is one of the many reminders. In the same way that a child must not be given more than can be physically handled, God protects and instructs us in the same way. When we prove that we are ready for more, He blesses us with more, and not a moment before that time.

Proverbs 3:9-10 9 Honor the Lord with your wealth and with the best part of everything you produce. 10 Then he will fill your barns with grain, and your vats will overflow with good wine.

Jesus Christ deserves our absolute best of everything we have to give. So many people think this only applies to our finances, and still are hesitant. It specifically says "everything". Our best ideas and projects should also be for God's glory and honor. Then, as it also clearly states, will we receive wine and grain (things we want and things we feel we need), and not just in small doses but full and overflowing.

XI Parting Words

When all else fails, remember...

Deuteronomy 6:5 You shall love the Lord your God with all your heart, with all your soul, and with all your strength.

Fill your heart with love for the Lord. If you do so, it will be impossible to have hate, envy, lack of forgiveness or any other negative emotion or action in your heart at the same time. Let your future and your dreams be larger that any one person, issue or circumstance that stands in your way.

Romans 8:28 And we know that all things work together for good to those who love God, to those who are the called according to His purpose.

No matter what happens in your business, stay focused on God and His purpose and promise for your life. There will be ups as well as downs. Things will always come together and work out just fine. Worry is the opposite of faith, so if you are worried, you are lacking in faith. Trust that everything will always be fine. There is a lesson in all things.

Colossians 3:17 And whatever you do in word or deed, do all in the name of the Lord Jesus, giving thanks to God the Father through Him.

Rise above the obstacles. Always remember that you are a spiritual being having a natural experience. Let your life be an example of the love and power of God. Give thanks for everything, good, bad or indifferent.

Psalm 119:105 Your word is a lamp to my feet and a light to my path.

This is the beginning of an amazing, life-transforming journey. When things are great, come to the word. When all else fails, rejoice in the word. In everything that you do, rely on the word of God to direct you. Let His word guide you through this journey and throughout the rest of your days.

XII Excuses Be Gone: Affirmations that will retrain your brain

It is so important to create a habit of thinking positively and erasing the negative thoughts that invade your mind. Please understand the process of sowing and reaping. It applies to thoughts just as much as it does to the earth. Don't allow negative thoughts to take root in your mind. Learn to combat those negative thoughts immediately and replace every one with something positive. Don't just casually say them to yourself or make a robotic declaration out of habit. When you say each one, feel it, believe it, KNOW it as the truth for your life.

I am tired.

I have more than enough time, energy and resources.

I do not have enough money.

I have more than enough money and it comes to me easily. I invest, tithe, save and spend my money wisely.

They probably don't have the money.

I am attracting people who see the value of my business and can afford to invest in themselves.

It costs too much money to run my business.

I have the funds and resources necessary to invest in my business and in myself.

I don't know enough people.

I know all the right people and I add new people to my network everyday.

I don't know the right people.

I meet positive, successful, productive people everyday.

My family and friends are not supporting me.

I have the active support of everyone I need.

The meeting is too far.

I have the time and ability to be where I need to be, in order to build my business and improve my skills.

I won't have any guests at the meeting.

I attend all events with teammates that are looking to grow personally and professionally.

I will start going to meeting when the money starts rolling in.

I see the value of training and I do what it takes to get the information and training I need.

No one on my team is coming to the convention.

My entire team sees the value in attending the trainings that lead to the success they desire to achieve.

My customers are falling off.

I am grateful for every customer I have and know that more will come at just the right time.

People just don't seem interested.

There are so many people looking for what I have to offer. The Lord will have our paths to cross at exactly the right place and time.

No one wants to hear what I have to say.

The Lord is leading me to the people with whom I should be speaking. I offer relevant information that always manages to fall on exactly the right ears.

I am _____ (too old, too young, not smart enough, fill in the excuse).

I am enough. God created me, and what He creates is perfection.

I don't like talking on the telephone or talking to people.

I do what is necessary to build my empire.

I don't know who to call, what to say or what to do.

God orders my steps. My daily activities are productive and measurable. I readily share my business and God's blessings with people I meet and know.

I have talked to everyone I know.

I meet interested, interesting people everyday who inquire about what I do and how I can help them.

I don't know if this is for me.

The Lord brought me to this place for a reason. I am blessed in my situation and am a blessing to others.

Closing

It is my sincere hope and prayer that you have found value within these pages. Hopefully, you were reminded of scriptures that you, too, hold dear or maybe even added a few to your list. May the affirmations stick with you and become a part of your day. May God continue to bless you, your family, your business partners and your customers or clients.

Best wishes,

Ahesha

References:

New King James Version. Tennessee: Thomas Nelson Publishers, 1982. Print.

If you'd like to book Ahesha Catalano for a speaking engagement or get more information on her one-on-one or group training sessions, or her additional services, please visit: www.TheTravelDame.com

Thank you for your purchase, and remember to live the life you love and love the life you live.

God bless you!

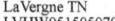
www.ingramcontent.com/pod-product-compliance
Lightning Source LLC
LaVergne TN
LVHW051505070426
835507LV00022B/2929